nature
therapy

scott stillman

nature therapy

wild soul press

durango, colorado

ISBN: 979-8-9892844-3-6

without wilderness
we create our own prison
boxing ourselves in from all sides

contents

we worry about so much

when freedom is

right outside

the door

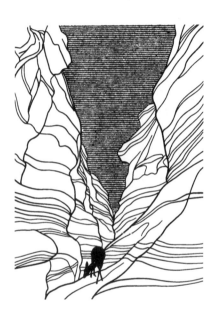

descent

i feel like i'm getting
close to something
but what?

maybe it's an end or new beginning
a crossroads or time to choose
but choose what?

maybe it's time to give up
latch onto a feather in the wind
set sail on the breeze

life...
is it a struggle or a breeze?

lately, i seem to be choosing *struggle*
a complex web of thoughts and ideas
crashing into each other all at once

i feel myself drifting further and further
into the black hole of incessant mind noise

———

in attempting to connect us all
through electronics
we have succeeded
in universal disconnect

the constant alerts that beg
every last drop of attention
rob us from any connection
we had in the first place

the moment has been lost
we are all trying to find it
searching for the only thing
we know is truly *real*

———

our mind-dominated world
is one of straight lines
boxes, and grids

every last scrap of awareness
sucked out by an ever-expanding army
of glowing rectangles

at times when i close my eyes
they are all i can see

i can feel it happening to myself
walking down the street
a zombie among the walking dead

who are all of these people?
what are they doing?
who am i?
have we all forgotten?

then i know it's time
to leave this world—
just temporarily

taking sanctuary
to the mountains and deserts
back of beyond, where the pavement ends
to wilderness, *the gateway to the soul*

———

solo backpacking
is my time to reboot

step outside the real world
stop talking
stop thinking
start *listening*

it's a time for gratitude and healing
both spiritual and physical

it's a time to walk
one foot in front of the other
and breathe in deep blissful silence

it will take a few days
for my busy mind to slow its chatter
but it always does

so long as i'm patient
trust the process
and submit completely to a power
much greater than myself

———

our society is one
of quick fixes

there's a pill for depression
a gadget for boredom
social media for loneliness
the pub for sadness

when i get lonely
what's really happening?
where do i feel loneliness in my body?

most people never give themselves the chance
to ask these questions

at the first itch of loneliness
we pick up the phone
log onto the internet
knock at the neighbor's door
or start a project

how about boredom
depression
anger
sadness?

we run

we're afraid of being with our emotions
we're afraid of being with ourselves

———

who am i when i take away my gadgets?
my friends and family?
my activities and job?
my status and gender?
my name?

who am i???

questions like these haunt us
especially as we get older

who we think we are
and who we really are
are often two very different things

we believe that we are our story
everything in our lives leading up to now
we believe we are our past
but if we take away our story

what's left?

———

why am i forever infatuated
with going deeper?

constantly peeling back the linoleum
clawing through surface
trying to find some semblance of meaning

something to penetrate the illusion
of our regimented world

hunting for scraps of truth
morsels of magic
traces of wisdom
anything to prove we mustn't work so hard

just to be *okay*

———

the cold truth is—we don't matter
no more than a bug, a rock
or a tree matters

in this vast inclusiveness
we are all equal parts
and this is entirely the point
to be part of the shebang

not to live separate closed-off lives
or to live the longest
or acquire the most
or domesticate the earth
but to be part of the whole experience

to suggest otherwise is simple delusion

———

we think we have freedom
but are we truly free?

how many of us can choose
what we want to do tomorrow?

most of us are locked into our schedules
chained to our routines

freedom has become a myth
a distant dream
some ideological notion we long for
yet rarely obtain

working through our prime sitting at desks
staring at computer screens
wasting away our youth so that someday
if we work hard enough
if we save enough
if the stock market doesn't crash
we might retire on a beach
or a cabin by the lake
or for those with less demanding tastes
in our own homes

then, in our golden years
we shall finally have the freedom
to do as we please

write our own schedules
live by our own rules

if we live that long
which is not certain

can't i live while i'm young?

———

must we eternally dwell
in fear of early death
while simultaneously fearing
a life too long?

we worry we will die early
missing out on all the things
we long to do

or that our money pile will run out
leaving us to starve elderly in the streets

we've become paranoid
worrying about everything
except for what's in front of us

life happens now—
it will never happen yesterday
and as we well know
tomorrow never comes

until we realize this glaringly obvious fact
we'll continually be striving
for something we can never have

running in circles
chasing our own tails
working to make as much money as possible
so that someday we can finally be free

———

the world stirs—
traffic jams, accidents, murder, rape
but the desert sits
oblivious to the madness

a cricket chirps
a bat flutters
and the sky grows silent with stars

a lone aspen sings her lonely song
inaudible to the rest of the world

humans may have taken over the earth
but these pockets
these sanctuaries—*remain*

———

when we eat ourselves to obesity
resorting only to our electronic devices for entertainment
gorging on images of death and violence
while simultaneously pretending to shun both

when we become sloths
existing only to multiply
dominating every species
claiming every piece of god's green earth
as private property

when we become a *disease*—

we will be eradicated
exterminated
like a termite infestation

then the earth shall go on without us
just as before
until a new species comes along

so the cycle continues...

———

as much as we feel in control
mother nature has the upper hand

she, like always
shall determine our fate

———

we are chained to our pasts
haunted by things we cannot change

the race of our ancestors
the country of our birth
the genetics of our parents

forced to play the cards we are dealt
we carry these heavy loads on our backs
for the rest of our lives

only the animals run free
unhindered by borders, fences
walls, property lines
imaginary dividers that have no meaning
history that contains no relevance

———

nature passes
no judgment

we are all
just passing through

struggling to live
destined to die

———

we are born with playfulness—
and play we will
until we're taught that life is serious
there are very important things to be done
and we must focus not on the present
but on the future

happiness is stolen from us
and projected to an imaginary place
that we can never reach

we become lost in the illusion
that happiness resides in the future

a practical joke
we've played on ourselves

———

our civilized world is not reality
but a game we play

existing so we can pack
millions into a tiny area

complete with electricity and indoor plumbing
restaurants and beer gardens
movies and bookstores
cars, trucks, buses
subways, and airplanes

it exists for our amusement
and there is nothing wrong with it
so long as we realize that the real world is *outside*
with the rest of nature

and should be treated as such

———

when we start to take
our thoughts too seriously
this is when we lose grasp

we fall into disillusion
identifying ourselves
with the complexities of the mind

the human brain was intended
to be used as a tool
so we could hunt, fish
gather nuts and berries, build shelters
fight off attackers, stay alive

when there is no longer a need to hunt
build our own homes, or fight—
our minds begin to wander

the tool has been left unattended

let it go too long
and the brain becomes a monster
attaching itself to every whim, every desire
every problem, anything at all

———

the problem with not knowing what you want
is that you want *everything*

so we spend, spend, spend
on every little thing
we think will bring us happiness

of course happiness never comes
because we never actually asked ourselves
what we wanted in the first place

we're like ships sailing
the open seas without a compass

changing course every time
we think we see land

————

life is a harrowing adventure
of ups and downs, twists and turns
intense joy and blood-curdling fear

the key is knowing
how to steer the ship
during the storms

if you don't know where you're headed
the storm may take you someplace
you don't want to go

storms can be opportunities
so long as you don't get stuck in the troughs
troughs are necessary
but the crest will always come

that's when you need to be ready
or you'll miss your opportunity entirely

so is life—
a wave that builds and crashes
over and over again

the key is learning to *surf*
there's magic behind every swell
but if you're too oblivious to notice
you'll miss it every time

———

you cannot step onto any one peak
and stay there forever
nor would you want to
after a while you'd become bored

the only way to get to the next peak
is back down into the valleys
the dark woods, the lonely forest

then it's another grueling climb
back to the top

life is about *change*
not staying in one place all the time
yet this is exactly what we do

we find one level of happiness
we are comfortable with
and throw out the anchor
working our tails off to stay on that one peak
forgetting that we were born with two legs to roam

and the world is full of endless peaks!

———

it's simply not possible
to grab onto any one moment in time
and stay there forever

life moves
time moves

if we fight it
we suffer

———

forsake nature
and forsake yourself
renouncing your own mother

doomed to be eternally lost
in the mindless pursuit of soulless desire

the great illusion of modern times

———

if there is anything that causes suffering
it's our constant desire for something else

to feel different than we feel
to be somewhere other than where we are

we are constantly saying *no* to life
that it's not good enough

that we want something better

———

most of us will never
know of real struggle

grumbling about the economy
while sitting in the warmth of our homes

our cabinets stocked with food
complaining there's nothing to eat

———

if we tame the last wild places
truth will be lost

leaving us trapped inside our own game
of winners and losers, competition and greed

trampling one another
in our own imagined race to the top
all so we can finally
win the game of happiness

but there is no game to be won
no happiness to be found
no reward for our needless suffering
in our imaginary future

just a dead end, an illusion
a big prank we played on ourselves

———

trust mother nature
and she'll show you her secrets

spite her and she'll
turn an indifferent hand

leave you to the vultures

———

we are children playing with toys
thinking our childish game
is the real world

how insignificant we've become
no longer able to hear the music of life
too selfish to even listen

we've deemed ourselves 'too important'
too busy to play in the dance of life

nature has been reduced to a static backdrop
for our all-consuming human activity

a pile of resources to be exploited
and serve the needs of humanity alone

a nice place for a picnic
when we are finished doing more important things

if we have time

we've forgotten that everything in nature
affects everything else

every action has consequence
good, bad, or indifferent

it's all there in the message
if we care to listen

———

we are born as pure love
then we get too smart for our own good

educated by our elders
that feelings aren't to be trusted
happiness lies in the future
and we are separate from what surrounds us

we stop seeing the rocks, trees, bugs
and other animals as our friends

further we drift from our true identities
and nature further into the background
until we no longer notice it

then on occasion
while experiencing a rare glimpse of unspoiled beauty
we wallow up

remembering for a split-second
how beautiful and magical it all was

before we had to *grow up*

———

humans are born with an extraordinary gift:
the ability to travel in our minds

our incredible imaginations
allow us to create vivid fantasies
about the past and future

we've become so good at this
that we believe these fantasies to be real

many have gone so far
as to live in this state all the time

while such a condition
might otherwise be considered *delusional*
this has become reality for millions of people
many would even consider it normal

it is anything but

while past and future projection are useful tools
if left unattended they can cause
entire civilizations to lose grasp on reality

the side effects of which are severe
including depression, drug and alcohol addiction
even suicide

when the affected individual
finally gets relief from this terrible affliction
they feel an immediate high

like experiencing sudden liberation
from chronic pain

or waking up from a bad dream

———

as much as we try
to cling to the shore

the river of life
flows

we forget that the ground beneath our feet
is not steady but hurling through space
at unfathomable speeds

with each passing year
the moon drifts further away
the earth's rotation slows
and our days get progressively longer

as our climate warms
the oceans are advancing
coming back to reclaim the land

wash away our sins

———

the world doesn't need saving
there's only saving ourselves

we've removed ourselves
from the pulsing rhythms of life

powerful technology has brought us
to this unparalleled brink in time
where mother nature barely recognizes
us as her own

looking down upon earth from outer space
we must look like aliens

an invasive species
festering on the land

———

our species has become overwhelmed
exhausted, overstimulated

everyone in a hurry
to get nowhere

meanwhile
nature never rushes
yet everything is accomplished

———

when life drags on
to the point where we start thinking—
is this all there is?

we've reached
the end of the road

the solution is simple
take another road

———

our emotions
have become chaotic

elated one moment
depressed the next

everything determined
by what's flashing
on screens before our eyes

a literal roller coaster
of random thoughts

———

we think we have individuality
but this is hardly the case

millions march to the beat of the same drum
thinking the same thoughts
craving the same gadgets
wandering in the same aimless fashions

we set goals we think are unique
but prove to be little more
than variations of the same theme
always based on what society wants us to crave

individuality is thrown by the wayside
as we become groomed
conditioned, tenderized, desensitized

like cows in line
for the slaughterhouse

———

with or without us—

there is no pause
in the singing of birds
the blowing of winds
the breaking of waves
the ebbing and flowing of tides

———

we strive to save the manatee
the sea turtle, the snow leopard
the spotted owl

how about the human?
this strange species that reproduces
with wild abandon and destroys
everything in its path

are we noble creatures
or an invasive species?

what purpose do we serve?

what would stop mother nature
from pulling the plug altogether?

———

in this river of life that flows
what is this desperation
to cling to the shore?

———

we are born knowing the secret of life
we just can't say it

when we grow up and learn to speak
we forget what we wanted
so desperately to say

———

in the end we are equal
like the birds, the snakes
the rats, and the worms

we are born with nothing
we die with nothing

it's what happens in-between
that counts

———

your heart is beating
will it beat tomorrow?
who knows?

life is a mystery
it's time to start treating it that way
the only irresponsible thing you can do is waste it

you are here
god only knows why
but you have the dreams
and desires you do for a *reason*

the truth is
you do know why you're here
the problem is society wants your dreams
to fit into some preconceived mold

it all goes back to that
high school guidance counselor—

"what do you want to be when you grow up?"

whoever said
we wanted to grow up?

growing up is *killing us*

———

when we stop seeing
the world
as a playground

nature
as a classroom

beauty
in the mundane

we perish

———

growing up is like dying
and going to heaven
enjoying it for a while
then deciding all this holiness
is a bit dull and we should get on to
more important things

as we concern ourselves
with these so-called important things
we further distance ourselves
from the heaven we were born into

until we *forget* we're there

let me clue you in on a little secret
shh. don't tell anyone...

you're in heaven now

———

whatever we focus on becomes energized

if we focus on our problems
our problems become energized
they get bigger, more complex, all-consuming

focus on all the reasons you can't do something
and those reasons will reinforce themselves

focus on the fact that you're depressed
and you'll become more depressed

focus on what's wrong with the world
and you'll find more that's wrong with the world

this kind of thinking
easily becomes a never-ending
downward spiral of negativity and doubt
leading to depression and mental illness
even suicide

we think the universe is so complex
but it's actually quite simple

it gives us precisely what we think about

———

a squirrel focuses on the nut
so it gets the nut

a bird focuses on the worm
so it gets the worm

humans do not operate
so simply

rather than focusing on the nut
we focus on all the problems
that could go wrong trying to obtain the nut

so that's exactly what we get
more problems

why not focus on the nut?

———

when an animal becomes sedentary
it sends signals that things are bad

that it's old or sick or starving
that it's time to die

when we are sedentary
we send out those same signals

without even knowing it

———

just because we think
we ought to help others
doesn't mean we have something to give

our best teachers lead by example

likewise, we cannot expect to help others
until we've found happiness *ourselves*

———

happiness means
something different to us all

i cannot know what makes you happy
you cannot know what makes me happy
that's what makes us unique

the problem is we have this
one-size-fits-all approach

this explains why the prescribed life—
school, job, house, family
consumerism, retirement, death—
leads to so much anxiety and depression

that formula works for some
but not for all

we are all different
each with unique dreams and desires

these dreams and desires
make the world go 'round

if we all wanted the same thing
life would be pretty dull

———

society is constantly pushing us
toward a kind of dreaded socialism
that dissolves uniqueness and individuality
into a colorless mass

we've seen where such practices lead

hitler thought he was improving society
so did stalin and countless others

throughout history, terrorists, cults
and religions have performed unthinkable acts
thinking they were *improving* the world

i cannot improve you
no more than you can improve me

we are perfect as we stand

———

suppose the sun stopped shining
deeming itself overly selfish
just beaming all the time
and not contributing *more* to the world

suppose bees stopped gathering nectar
feeling guilty *taking* from the flowers

suppose clouds stopped providing rain
thinking they should help the planet
in some *other* way

the world would fall apart

nature works *because* it is selfish
it is selfish by design

it is we who second-guess
our dreams

when we stop following our dreams
we let the whole world down

———

the universe knows no distinction
between a big goal and a small one

it's we who judge our dreams

setting the parameters
on what we think we deserve

———

growing up is just another
name for copping out
giving up, throwing in the towel

when we're young
the world is mysterious and unknown
when we grow up
we become know-it-alls

nothing feels new anymore
because we think we know
how the world works

this is gibberish

we can never understand the universe
any more than we can understand
where we came from
and where we'll go when we die

life is a mystery
that's what makes it worth the ticket

———

it's normal to crave security
yet by nature, life is insecure

the only thing we can count on is *change*
so we must become adaptable

———

wilderness is our only hope
our final lifeline to reality

everything that is true and wild and free

when wilderness disappears
there will be no hope left
for the human race

extinction will be the only way
a social experiment gone awry
and the earth shall go back to the way it was

before we paved paradise
and put up a parking lot

———

i know that i am confined
to the modern world
and must adhere to its rules
to reap the comforts that society provides

yet i refuse to buy into them completely
i do not want to become *dependent*

once that line is crossed
dependency becomes a crutch

———

day by day, moment by moment
we choose love or hate
life or death
light or darkness

the seeds for both
are contained within all things
both living and nonliving

focus on beauty and beauty you find
focus on darkness and darkness will prevail

beauty guides through the heart
darkness through the mind

———

if we are not living our truth
are we not living a lie?

our inner child knows this all too well
crawling deeper and deeper
into the far corners of our beings
until we finally find truth

or we stop looking altogether
forsaking our inner child
allowing the pure essence of our very soul
to stay hidden for eternity
or at least until we die

and then we do die
lonely and afraid
repeating the process over and over

until we finally *get it*

———

i'm blessed and cursed
with the soul of a child

one who is easily distracted, easily bored
and prone to depression if this
goes on too long

yet when i nourish
that inner child

my delight astonishes even myself

———

as far as i travel
as deep into the wilderness as i push
there i always am

just the same

searching for something out *there*
that i already know is inside of me

something out *there*
to remind me that there is more to life
than what i can see on the surface

something to remind me
who i really am

———

we are born searching
constantly seeking something
we cannot name

something we want so desperately
but cannot describe

out here in the wilderness
that searching is gone

gone like a *bad dream*

———

can i survive in a busy world
of schedules, deadlines
payments, and obligations?

will i remain part
of the flow of the universe?

or will i fall back into the
hustle and bustle of city life
feeling myself separate once again?

time will tell

———

i must remind myself that everything
is working perfectly according to plan

but i also need to keep things in *balance*
make sure there's not too much yin
and not enough yang

otherwise i'll need to make a change

———

many of us have had revelations of *truth*

perhaps in a church or monastery
or high on a mountaintop
or gazing into the eyes of a newborn baby

that experience when we stop thinking
for just a moment
and suddenly know some overwhelming truth
that we cannot put to words

but these moments are fleeting

as soon as we try to put them to words
or label them in some way
we lose grasp

we are back to thinking again
the moment is lost

truth is enough
just knowing that it exists

so long as we don't try
to turn it into something

some *thing*
which it is not

———

always we want something else

we're sad and we wish to be happy
we're cold and we wish to be hot
we're in one place and we wish to be in another

does our pain really come from our situation
or from our constant desire for something else?

are we not just running in circles
chasing our own tails?

must we always be chasing
the next *better* moment?

as fast as we try to run
can we ever get to the future?

what if now is all we ever have?

a movie with no beginning
no end

———

don't be one way
wishing for another

only to arrive at the new way
wishing for the first

———

i am not these cravings
i am not these emotions
i am not these mood swings
i am not these hopes
i am not these fears
i am not these pleasures
i am not these sufferings

i'm just along for the ride

———

i think it's cold
but who would know?

the air is so still
temperature cannot be felt

then there's this silence
screaming into my ears

there's no escape

i drop something on the rock beside me
to break the silence—
my spoon

the screaming ceases
then nothing

a slight breeze from some far-off place
stings my face

yes
it's cold

with the breeze
comes the hollow
sound of the night

darkness
cold
winter

———

my world closes off
as i wind my way through dense tunnels
of decaying forest
twisted tree trunks and roots
wet marshes and bogs

the air becomes eerie quiet
just the sound of my footsteps
my labored breathing
my steady beating heart

the noises sound unnatural
and out of place
like an intrusion on the silence

everything sounds out of proportion
i think i hear a raging waterfall
a crashing in the forest
but it's just my pack brushing my shoulders
my boots on the trail

my labored breathing

———

it starts to rain

large drops pelt me in the head
like insults

next comes the thunder
lashing out coldly
illuminating the canopy of trees above
then fading to black

another flash cracks loudly through the trees
directly above my head

darkness, more rain
the *dark night of the soul*

———

i'm way back inside my head—

a tangled mess of thoughts
bouncing all around

a downward spiral
of negativity and doubt

gray clouds compound and coalesce
then fold back in on each other
swelling like seas in a violent storm

i come to a bluff
and stare up into the sky

there is something up there
trying to get out

the clouds split open
instead of more darkness
a patch of blue is revealed
a single ray of light escapes

raindrops transform into falling diamonds
peaks turn to gold
i'm transported to another world
a mystical fairyland

my thoughts freeze as mother nature
whips me back to the present moment
back to the *now*

with another crescendo
my patch of blue collapses
swelling back into grayness

darkness returns
the rain continues
the forest closes in on me again

———

the rain continues
heavy and ferocious
large drops beat the roof of my tent
i feel like i'm inside of a drum

this goes on for hours
as i lie on my back
in a chamber of sound

feelings of loneliness
cravings for soft skin
soothing music
cold beer

the cravings will pass
try to *stay in the moment*

———

thunder barrels
through the canyons
echoing off the walls
of petrified skyscrapers

rain pounds
against tent fabric
saturating my dreams
in an ocean of sound

the storm is alive
a living, raging organism

rather than a witness
i feel myself part of it

i'm no longer sure what's real
and what's fantasy

where the dream ends
and reality begins

or if there's even a difference

———

memories flash through my head
from some other world

a child in a plastic kiddie pool
a teen at a high school dance
a businessman wearing a tie

i try to piece together the details
build a timeline
tell the story

the story?
it unravels in my fingers

the hand of time ticks
i hold tightly to the needle
i don't want to miss an instant

that's where it *all happens*

———

we've civilized ourselves quite well
removing ourselves almost entirely
from the natural landscape
all for the modern comforts of civilization

it's no wonder we're so *restless*

these wild places
were a part of us for generations

they're in our blood

———

there's a lot
to explore

and time
is running out

———

go now—
leave your cubicle
your private office
your steady paycheck
your *benefits* package

what's the benefit of sitting all day
inside a climate-controlled box
forty hours a week
fifty weeks a year

just to come home
to another insulated box to
eat, sleep, repeat?

the real world is outside
away from our man-made cells
of concrete and steel

it's out *there*

———

like medusa
she seduces me

provocative shapes and colors
tempting me onto the desert rock
the sizzling stone, the crackling dirt
the hot silence

tempting death
promising eden

the holy grail
the hanging garden
the oasis in the lost city of stone

on the fringes of society
far from industry
developments
progress

it's out there
i just know it

i've been there before

———

we can only take so much civilization
before it *gets* to us

then it's time to get back
to where it all begins

———

there is a way out
an emergency escape
a backdoor exit

it's called *wilderness*

———

the more we simplify
the freer we become

the freer we become
the less we cling

the less we cling
the closer we are to god

until we finally reach the end of our days
standing at the precipice of life
staring out into the face of the unknown

then we shall be ready
to hurl ourselves into the great abyss
stripped bare of money, possessions
clothes, skin and bones

free
free at last

———

we don't know what we're missing
until we step outside the illusion
and discover that pristine
version of ourselves

the only one
that matters

everything else is *noise*

———

how strange that we sacrifice
so much for our careers
as if they were the most
important things in life

yet we are careless
with our free time

the only thing
we know for a fact to be finite

———

how enlightening must it be
to see through the eyes of an eagle
rabbit, mountain lion, or snake?

i find it impossible
not to regard these fellow creatures
as enlightened beings

they truly know the joys
of simplicity

they do not carry
this human *disease*

which compels one to endure
such a stressful existence

———

we are an uncanny species—

terrified of dying too early
petrified of living too long

if we die too young
we miss out on retirement

if we live too long
we exhaust our savings

either way we lose

this deranged fear
must be unique to humans

the rest of nature appears
to live entirely in the
present moment

across the animal kingdom
death is so prevalent
so absolutely certain
that it's a normal part of existence

at any moment
an animal knows it could be eaten
must be eaten!
in order for the broader scope of life to go on

death is not a problem
it's a simple fact of life

———

we make our lives unstable
by layering on too many complexities

fundamentally, humans are not so different
from the rest of nature's creatures

food, water, and a warm
place to sleep are all we need
this is what nature *intended*

is happiness buying every gadget
that pops up on our social media feed
and having it delivered to our front door
in less than forty-eight hours?

or is happiness being content
with the simple pleasures
that nature freely provides?

i don't see many
content people nowadays

what i see is longing, craving
desperation

this is capitalism functioning at its best
and it's the opposite of happiness

the constant advertisements
that bombard our devices
keep us in a never-ending state of unfulfillment

we are running on hamster wheels
chasing that dangling carrot
of future happiness

———

even the darkest of places
contain the seed of light

———

how many of us walk around
looking for differences
rather than commonalities—

when what we need most
is someone different than ourselves?

someone to *compliment*
not mirror our own personalities

yet this is exactly who we push away

by doing so—
we become more and more entrenched
in our own narcissistic ways

———

if human beings have one major flaw
it's our tendency to separate ourselves
into groups and pit one against the other

throughout history
dividing and conquering
has always been the way

we do this disturbingly well
down to the least common denominator
dividing until there's no one left
but carbon copies of ourselves

that's where the loneliness sets in
the depression

we start to see everyone
outside our segregated circles
as so different from us
that we lock ourselves into isolation

fearing strangers, trusting no one

if we could only see
that all humans share
the same common enemy

and it's none other
than this terrible disease itself
that compels us to divide

if humanity could realize
we share this common threat
we could start the next revolutionary war

not a war against each other
but a war on *division* itself

———

our planet is not dying
but constantly being reborn
for she is young and full of vigor

at any moment, she shall say *enough!*
shaking us off like fleas
from a dog's behind

whether through a tsunami
an earthquake, an asteroid
or some other natural occurrence

time will tell

it has happened before
it shall happen again

ah, but the billion-dollar
question is when?

no one knows

a child may die in infancy
or live to be a hundred

this is the great mystery of life

would we want it any other way?
could it be any other way?

———

society tells us that life is expensive
when in truth, all we need are basic foods
and a warm place to sleep

we make our life choices
each has its consequence

most either trade time for money
or money for time

the question comes down to
which is more valuable?

———

what is all this fighting
the present moment?

what is all this wishing away
the only thing in life
that actually exists?

all for the sake of projecting
some imaginary *better* moment
that only exists in our minds?

who among you
is truly suffering?

are you without clothes
or shelter or food or water?

we complain about our circumstances
as if we're owed something better
while the deer and antelope
are content with what nature
freely provides

when is the last time you saw a depressed deer?
a moping mountain lion?
a suicidal squirrel?

it is *we* who inflict our sufferings
upon ourselves

constantly judging and comparing
our lives to our neighbors
who are invariably better off than we—

having fancier smartphones, larger houses
higher paying jobs, more well-behaved children
more attractive spouses, happier childhoods
brighter futures, and so on

hogwash!

human problems, all of them
not to be taken seriously
in a world with *real concerns*

our problems are invented
by the irrational mind and its incessant tendency
to analyze, scrutinize, criticize, ostracize

this great mental illness that plagues humanity
blinds us from the divine perfection
of the present moment

the only moment that ever was
the only moment that ever will be

———

all that stuff society says we need—
it's a hoax

do you think primitive cultures
considered themselves poor?

we must look like tycoons by comparison!

how much satisfaction must they have had
hunting their food, growing their vegetables
building their homes, making their garments
shaping knives, spears, arrows
and axes by hand?

how much satisfaction must they have felt
sitting down to food on their table
with a roof over their heads
without so much as a penny
to their names?

undoubtedly, they would laugh
at our civilized culture
that relies on clocks
to tell us when we're hungry
and weather apps
to tell us if it's raining outside

they would see us as *crazy people*
lost inside a silly game of our own invention

———

i refuse to succumb to this
deranged human fear of living too long
while simultaneously fearing an early death

i choose to live my life
always in the present

when i'm an old man
what will i truly need anyway?

a shack in the woods
with a small garden
to grow my vegetables?

for the love of god—
save me from the long, cruel demise
of decaying inside some expensive
long-term health care facility

eating microwaved meals
breathing sterilized air
watching reruns of *dynasty*

let me die peacefully
under wide open skies

one can always dream...

———

when we destroy our natural landscapes
we do so for money

when we spend our precious days
staring at computer screens
we do so for money

the reason we have war and crime
and hate and greed—
all because of money

whenever we buy into this mentality
we keep the delusion alive

the *myth* that money buys happiness

of course, money can be fun
it can be fun!

but like most things
the accumulation of money
has a diminishing return

we can only improve our lives so much
before it becomes an endless addiction

grasping for tiny scraps of happiness
in an endless stream of amazon boxes
or home improvement projects

this kind of happiness is as fleeting
as a drunk's stupor
leading only to headaches
and long-term unfulfillment

yet the addiction is mighty strong
and so we drink anyway
squeezing every last drop of happiness
out of each hard-earned dollar

all the while
true happiness has been
free for the taking

always has been
always will be

———

the ability to think only when we wish
has become a rare skill

when our minds are chronically clouded
with meaningless worries and trivial concerns
we're perpetually exhausted

then when a real problem arrives
we're overwhelmed with indecision

———

our human world is a mess
it's been a mess for a very long time

at the center of our problems
is this peculiar gene all humans have

that which divides and dissects
judges and labels
skepticizes and doubts

is there any doubt in the bobcat's mind
that she should eat the rabbit?

any doubt that the rabbit
should eat the grass?

any doubt that the grass
should feed on the soil?

humans are so disconnected from nature
we have no clue what we're supposed to be doing

so we spend our time
making widgets and atom bombs

———

if you must take me, mother nature
take me outside
with the rest of the animals
so that i might merge with creation

let me die empty handed—penniless!
under your blazing sun

not clutching my pocketbook
in some hospital bed
praying to some overpriced
medical apparatus to save my life

hoping for just one more day
beneath fluorescent lights

let me die with nothing between us
but *earth and sky*

———

there is
nothing left

but the hollow sound
of my own voice

strange
empty
insignificant

———

passage

an orange glow
creeps through the fog
spreading over my camp
like a warm fuzzy blanket

rocks radiate in mystical light
dampness clings to the air
a deep silence falls upon the land

my mind slows
stops

the first things to drop away are the names
i no longer see a rock, a lizard, a tree

i only see

———

i know that i must simplify
learn what it means to master being human
perfection in every step
no hesitation
no thought
no ego

———

i'm not here to tame or conquer
i'm here to connect
to find the *gateway*

i know it's out here

if i'm not careful
i could miss it

———

i inhale deeply
taking in the silence
until i can take no more

then i let it all out
everything
until there's nothing left

i wait
for what i don't know
but i wait

the light fades
ever so slightly

changing everything

clouds build
a bird chirps
another answers

———

if i were to die in this meadow
what would change?

the flowers will still blossom
the butterflies will still flutter
the hawks will still soar

but who to contemplate them?

perhaps a small child
in a similar meadow
on a similar day?

a sinking feeling
deep inside my gut

this body wants to survive
as all life wants to persevere

yet i can't help but wonder
if in our final moment
there is a surrender

if just before the rabbit
is eaten by the coyote
there is a flash of peace
a moment of understanding

a transformation will occur
but life will go on
just the same

when i sit and surrender to this moment
i know that as long as there is life
i too will exist

that i will go on
just the same

———

i fall asleep in the grass

the sounds of the creek carry me away
on a blanket of liquid dreams

———

the sound of running water
consumes me

i feel like i could sleep
for days

i have found refuge
i have found peace

deep within the cracks
of the earth

———

the breeze stops
stillness prevails
but the sound of water remains
it's a new kind of silence

this silence, it's everywhere
in the sound of thunder
on a busy street corner
the roar of a freight train

the key is to listen
to the silence behind the sounds

the silence within

———

if meditation is something you *do*
this is quite the opposite

there is no trying
no doing

just sitting, observing
stillness, splendor

i drift on the waves
of a mountain breeze

in the vapor
of a floating cloud

upon the wings
of a soaring hawk

energy buzzes through
my every cell

meditation—
one word, so difficult to define

is it to do or not to do?
latch onto or let go?

———

the land has opened up completely
revealing her most intimate secrets
her most sacred beauty

around every corner
blossoms a new landscape
each more magnificent than the last

———

beyond all else
we must remember who we are
where we come from
and where we shall return

there comes a time when
we must make our pilgrimage—

leave our houses
our cities of concrete and steel
and make our journey back to wilderness

back *home*

———

what is it about this place?
what is it about this desert?

i search for an answer
but come up dry
like always

there is something here beyond words
something *unexplainable*

a presence
something living, breathing, *listening*

this place is time
witnessing the rain, the wind
freezing and thawing

a canvas on which the earth paints its story
leaping from the landscape
saturating the senses
invoking the wildest of imaginations

art without the artist
painting without the painter
beauty for the sake of beauty

i walk gently onto the canvas
beginning to feel myself part of the piece

i'm here—not to dig and drill
excavate and haul away
probe and prod, measure and examine
rape and pillage, tame and conquer—
but to witness

to be in the presence of greatness

i want to listen
not to the desert
but along with her

i want to see
not only the rocks
but to see what they see

i want to experience
not just the beauty
but to become it myself

———

there's an all-knowingness out here
it lies within all this silence and stillness

a wisdom so profound it transcends words
an understanding so pure it cannot be explained

when i tap into this wisdom
a switch is flipped

my mind
always up front
driving and controlling everything
takes a back seat

and my soul
hiding quietly in the back seat
jumps up to take shotgun

like a domesticated wolf returned to the wild
a spark of energy rekindles my true nature

i remember
pause for a moment
then go bounding off into the wild

never to look back

———

my pen moves all by itself
across the paper
recording the moment
the great mystery

i'm trying hard to keep up
the facts, man
nothing but the facts

the truth!

with a trembling hand
and a tear in my eye
i now know
i finally understand

the truth is who i am

———

the boundaries between life
and death have grown blurry

no longer
can i tell the difference

an ancient tree stump is covered in moss
ferns grow out from the top

a downed log is blanketed
in tiny pink flowers

even the ground is alive
thick with spongy green plant life

mushrooms are everywhere
growing out of everything

rocks are covered in fuzzy
botanical gardens of their own
appearing as mounds of organic life

everything is intertwined
plants grow out of plants
trees grow out of trees

rather than competition
i see community
symbiotic relationships

never before has the circle of life
been so perfectly laid out before my eyes

there is no beginning, no end
no life, no death
just a natural flow

rather than a thousand species
i see only one—

earth species

———

where does one organism stop
and another begin?

what is what
and where do we draw the line?

how to make a separation?
without one we cannot have the other

without the decay
we cannot have new birth

a tree falls—crumbling to soil
nourishing ferns, lichens, mushrooms

these provide food for ants
beetles, tree frogs, salamanders

in turn, they provide food for owls
hawks, mountain lions, bears

they too die
feeding the vultures and ravens

finally worms turn their remains
back to soil

this cycle repeats itself over and over
so is the circle of life

in our cities of concrete and steel
we've removed ourselves
from these cycles

we've forgotten the circle of life—
the interconnectedness of all things

a shift in consciousness
is all that is required

life is abundant
with plenty to go around
until things fall out of balance

we will evolve or we will die

———

what are these mysterious flashes
in the heavens?

planets? ufos?
god winking at us from above?

i find it better not to know
to live in the mystery

what do we really
know anyway?

we give names to things
as if the names are a means to an end

but can we really
know a star?

do the letters s-t-a-r
describe the heavens
any more than the letters w-a-t-e-r
describe the ocean?

lose the words
and the mystery returns

———

no planes
no boats
no semis
no fed-ex trucks
no garbage trucks
no diesel trucks
no air conditioners
no construction vehicles
no busy highways
no generators
no motorcycles
no helicopters this morning

nothing but the wind
the howl of a coyote
my breath

———

we live in a noisy world
no wonder we're cursed
with the plague of incessant thought

fortunately, even the muddiest of waters
clear when stilled

as our world becomes increasingly
polluted with noise
silence is becoming
our rarest commodity

it hits like a freight train
when we find it

like a *wall of silence*

———

in wilderness
the sermon is delivered by no man

but rather by the rocks themselves
the air we breathe
the plants, the clouds
and the sky above

they regale a wisdom so ancient
so profound
that it permeates our souls deeply
using no words at all

free at last from the incessant rumble
of our busy world
the ancient wisdom of the earth
can finally be heard

sometimes resonating so deeply
that tears fill our eyes
love fills our hearts
and beauty blossoms from within

———

an hour passes
the croak of a raven
another hour

this much silence is intoxicating
it comes on like a drug
intensifying awareness
amplifying sound

it's the lack of sound
that's so deafening here
the absence of sound

my other senses become heightened
a phenomenon that must be experienced
to understand

with no sound at all
i focus on *nothing*

my mind becomes very, very still

———

the air vibrates with a buzz
that i can feel from the top of my head
to the bottom of my toes

love floods in
light is intensified
colors become more vivid
it becomes all-consuming
difficult to contain

can i love too much?
what will happen then?
i turn down the volume just a bit
more out of instinct than fear

the breeze picks up
giving me a sudden chill
i move into the sun and sit on a rock
the heat feels exhilarating

clouds build
thickening on the horizon

you've waited your whole life for this

no words
no words
no words

———

this is a museum
i am part of the exhibit
leaving my own footprints in the sand

everything has its story
some are hundreds of years old
others just minutes

it's *the greatest story ever told*

———

i could stay out here for weeks
if it weren't for the allure of such things as
cold beer in frosted pint glasses
burgers, fries, tacos

false promises, all of them
leaving me with a full belly
but empty soul

eternally unsatisfied
insatiably hungry
always wanting more, more, more

the next fix
an endless, maddening process

but i allow these things
to lead me back to civilization anyhow

i'm only human

———

as divided as we may seem
we're all in this together

in the end
there is no separateness

no lines drawn
between you, me
rock and tree

all of this i forget
over and over i forget

fortunately mother nature is patient
reminding me again each time
about the beauty, the silence, the light

and the miracle of all of existence

———

there is primal wisdom
deep within the fissures of earth

it's all right here
ready for anyone who wishes to learn

a truth that existed
long before our species arrived

one that will exist
long after we are gone

there is much to learn
so much to learn

i can feel it deep within the rock
away from the noise, pollution
and mindless chatter of incessant thought

the *madness* of our modern world

the world needs freaks
those who doubt conventional wisdom
question authority
and continually search for newer
better ways to live

freaks change the world

———

the time to live
can never be later

it must be *now*

———

the more we simplify
the richer we become

i'm not talking about money
i'm talking about *life*

———

hurry up!
time is of the essence

no one knows when you're going to die
so you'd better get busy living

why not do
something amazing?

———

refusing to grow up
is choosing to live

and experiencing every day
with the playfulness
and curiosity of a child

———

not growing up
means breaking the rules

rejecting society's unwritten laws
about how we should live our lives

it's about writing *your own story*

———

who wins the game of life?
those who die with the most money
or the biggest grin?

you cannot buy your dreams
only live them

———

sometimes we must
step off the trail
out of the rut
into the forest of dreams

———

you exist so the universe
can experience itself
only as it can through you

your uniqueness
is proof of that

to fight this uniqueness
is to deny the will
of the cosmos

———

opportunity exists in every moment
even the ones we perceive as *bad moments*

try accepting each moment
like you chose it yourself

life is a game and clues are everywhere
ignore them and get stuck

follow them to reach the next level
and the next
and the next...

———

when we begin
paying attention to life's clues
we develop a sort of sixth sense

instead of thinking our way through life
we *feel* our way through

no longer do we find the need
to debate everything

we're drawn to what feels right

———

when we surrender to the flow
we let go of any preconceived notions
of how we think things should play out
we let nature take the reins

this is how *miracles* happen

_____

life works in mysterious ways
when we hold on too tightly
we often sabotage what the universe
is trying to provide

look at a wild river on a map
it looks like chaos
but as we know
divine intelligence is at work

the river wants to make it to the sea
but a straight line
is rarely the path of least resistance

likewise, we need to know where we're heading
and trust the rest to divine unfolding

———

destinations are necessary
they keep us headed in the right direction

but between the dream
and the destination is life

the uncertainty is what makes it *worthwhile*

the best stories, as we know
are unpredictable

when the plot is expected
it's a sleeper
when laced with mystery
it's gripping

what kind of story do you want?
there are no wrong answers

you write the book

———

what do you want your life to look like?

once you know that
you can begin stripping away
all that is not your desire

then, when every last layer
has been removed
there will be your dream
sparkling like a diamond in the rubble

sadly, many leave their diamonds buried
working, working, working
trying to save enough money
so that someday they can live their dreams

but freedom doesn't come
from piling up a big heap of money

it comes from stripping away
peeling back
exposing what's buried beneath

———

in wilderness
we are immersed in truth

it becomes abundantly clear
that our pain derives
from our false sense of separation

here, that separation
is utterly and completely gone

gone like a bad dream

we're returned to our natural order
and place in the world

no better, no worse
but equal to everything else

with this grand indifference
comes radical inclusion
and i feel only love

love for the plants and flowers
chipmunks and hummingbirds
snakes and scorpions
seeps and springs
passing clouds
and rays of sunlight—my kin

like a long lost brother
i'm welcomed home

———

in the city—
our feelings of separateness are so prevalent
that they're contagious

even if we practice yoga
or meditate, or pray

feeling *one* with the infinite universe
for a few blissful uninterrupted moments

our feelings of separateness
creep right back in through the back door

in a world where everyone feels separate
it's simply too much to overcome

but in the forest—
i'm surrounded by trees
and they are enlightened!
and the rocks—enlightened!

among them
my state of disconnect is the exception
and i'm attuned to a broader perspective

welcomed into a new world

———

truth is silly, wise
profound

nature speaks a simple language
that gets right to the point

listen not with your ears
but with your heart

feel the love grow
then reciprocate

when you reciprocate
the love grows stronger
overflowing with truth

soon, all feelings of separateness will dissolve
as you reconnect with the world
you were born into

the one deep inside
you know is *real*

———

what we need is a revolution
a paradigm shift
a breakaway from technology
and reconnection with the natural world

for when we disconnect we *reconnect*
with the truth of who we are

nature will welcome us back
as she always does with open arms
we are part of her as she is of us

her love is so deep that it overflows our hearts
spreading out into the rest of the world

but don't take my word for it
i'm just a student

go see for yourself

leave your electronics at home
hike into a remote canyon
and sit, listen, wait

you may not feel anything at first
but just keep sitting. listening. waiting

eventually, after a few hours
a few days, a few weeks
you may start to feel something

shhh, listen...

it's in the rocks, the trees
the wind

———

i am here
not merely to survive
but to *live*

———

who is this maddening
over-analyzing entity inside my head?
surely we cannot be *related*

we drift apart
my mind and me
one watching the other

this *disconnect* is exactly what i needed

when we stop taking our thoughts so seriously
they lose their power
trailing off into some kind of distant
background noise

now there's nothing left but my footsteps
my steady beating heart

———

go ahead—
take risks, derail your routine
do something *amazing*

our species has it made
we're no longer fighting off predators
battling other tribes
or freezing to death

what exactly are we doing working forty
sixty, eighty hours a week
just to make a living?

if there is anything to fear
it is *time*

money can be replaced
time cannot

you can never get back lost time
time is priceless

———

no guru
no method
no teacher

come to the mountains
and the truth will find you

but if your mind is too busy
you will never hear it

if you're always trying to get somewhere
you will never get it

because here and now
is where it all lies

———

the ground is covered
not in grass but by tiny plants
glowing algae, and miniature forests of trees
and bushes only millimeters in height

when i look closer
there are even smaller plants
astonishingly perfect in symmetry
with little flowers growing out of them

if i had a microscope
we could go even further
revealing cells and atoms

until we reach that all-consuming *nothing*
that composes everything
that life-stuff we are all made of

there i find my truest self
in all that nothingness

i know that when i die
i will return to this place of nothingness

i'll lose this set of eyes
but an infinite number will remain

this is always the goal
to get down to nothing

because in all this nothing
lies the source of everything

and that dichotomy
is extraordinarily exciting!

———

in wilderness we see
the world as it truly is:

mountains, deserts, rolling plains
oceans with unfathomable depths
tropical islands and rainforests
animals, plants, and the earth—
a tiny speck of dust hurling through space
in a universe full of infinite galaxies
and all of this within an even larger void
of all-consuming nothingness

this is *reality*

not some idealistic fairytale
version of the world
but the real, actual truth

and it's spellbinding

―――――

in wilderness
we see that our lives
are utterly and completely meaningless
and in this we find *meaning*

the lesson is always the same:

we are born, we have a life, we die
so is the circular nature of being

this happens over and over
and no one is exempt

why not celebrate the inconceivable notion
that we get to witness it all

through our unique pair of eyes?

———

our minds function differently in the wild

not because they are switched off
but rather they are switched *on*

finally put to intended use

instead of wandering around aimlessly
in mindless thought
our minds are highly alert
standing guard
charged and ready for any task

solutions to problems come rapidly
and without waver

the brain becomes a powerful tool
solving problems as they arise
then waiting silently

on-call

ready for the next task
as per original design

―――――

sit in the forest long enough
and you begin to see
through animal eyes

as the fog of mindlessness starts to clear
thoughts flow away like water

cascading down the mountainsides
into the valleys

seeping into the soil
deep into the core of the earth

to be purified, cleansed
reborn into the world

———

when we learn to enjoy the climb
as much as standing on the peak
we are back into the flow

when we surrender to this flow
every moment becomes more enjoyable

things start to work out
because we are no longer fighting
our way upstream
but drifting with the current

life becomes a joyful journey
rather than a desperate search
for more highs and less lows

which is like fighting
life itself

when we surrender to the flow
we tune ourselves back in to nature

the problem is we *forget*
over and over we forget

that's why wilderness
is so important

we are students
and mother nature is our teacher

we must never stop learning
never stop attending her sermon

———

nature speaks a silent truth
beyond words and thought
transcending names, labels, science

the message is simple and pure
but when you try to define it
it vanishes into thin air

and in that vanishing
you find it again

like a beautiful butterfly
that can never be caught

try and catch her and she'll drive you mad
eluding you for all of eternity

but learn to fly with her
and all the wonders of the world
will be shown

and all the answers to your questions
be known

————

the very meaning of life
is held in nature's delicate silence

animals live in this silence all the time
as do the trees, the rocks, the sun
even the soil breathes this silence

it's *we* who bring
our noisy minds into nature

full of details, anxiety, and mindless chatter—
we carry the noise and clamor of the city

but if we learn to quiet our minds
and listen along with these silent beings
nature's silent message can finally be heard

———

the trees—
stand day after day
year after year, century after century
witness to all

soaking up life through their roots
inhaling through their leaves
and exhaling so that we too can breathe

trees are shining examples
of *being here now*

with nowhere to go, no wars to fight
no obligations, no deadlines to succumb to
each is a unique window unto the world
relinquishing truth to whoever wishes to listen

silent beings of awareness, energy, and light
messengers of peace, reason, and sanity

in a world slowly going insane

———

the rocks—
witness it all
through the eons of time
poised stately against deep blue sky
mighty watchmen presiding over the land

lifeless? hardly!
the rocks harbor the very wisdom
of the core of earth

emanating truth like an orchestra
a symphony, a resounding *wall of silence*

the rocks are the very foundation
on which we stand
to them we owe it all

if there is anything worth worshiping
it is the rocks

———

the sun—
beams down from above
a fiery ball of energy at the center of the universe
precisely aligned so that we may exist

any closer and we would burn
any further and we would freeze

if there is truly a god it is the sun
hanging in this delicate, perfect balance
shining her light, giving us life

reminding us each day
that we are the lucky ones

to be born on earth
is to be born in paradise itself

the sun says...

do you see how lucky you are?
every day i shine my light
so that you may live

go now and celebrate the day
play beneath my shining rays
and shine your own light i give you every day

spread the miraculous love
and beauty that is the earth

you are the reason that i shine
please don't box yourself in
set yourself free

this is your time to play in the forests
sing with the birds
frolic in the streams
swim in the oceans

sing, dance, shine like i do every day
without judgment, fear, hatred, or greed

earth is the most abundant of all planets
there is plenty to go around

———

money does not
buy peace of mind

detachment from money
buys peace of mind

when we simplify our lives
we regain the freedom we once had as children
but with the wisdom of age

when we are young
we have time but no money

when we are older
we have money but no time

it's never too late to jump back in
back to the childlike essence of our youth

there is a way out of our materialistic ways
it just takes a little *decluttering*

———

there is a method here
an ancient way of communication

i'd say *secret*
but it's no secret at all

the rest of nature understands it
perfectly fine

we've forgotten how to subdue our thoughts
and listen with feeling

the trees, the animals, the rocks
the sun and the moon
even the wind
they communicate in song

improvisational music
we can tap into anytime
if we listen with our hearts
and quiet our minds

this music invokes deep feeling
inside all those who listen

transmitting the *wisdom without words*

———

winter has returned
life has retreated and closed up tightly

one might say 'dead'
but the spark of life lies hidden beneath
ready to resurge when warm weather returns

the chatter of desert life has all but ceased
leaving nothing but the rocks
for they never sleep, never hibernate
never cease their soundless roar

the band has left the stage
leaving only the rocks to perform
their winter solo

in spring the full band shall reconvene
reuniting in grand concerto
celebrating their joyous return

the desert will once again
be wild with song

but for now it's just the rocks
humming together in a great hymn

i'm the lone observer—

audience of one
standing front and center
for the greatest show on earth

the price of admission costs nothing
but enduring the long dark night

now i'm first in line
for the rising of the sun
the thawing of the canyons
the cold hills, the frozen sand
my shivering bones

———

the rocks will swallow you up
in their vastness
take you into their world—
show you things

hold on tightly
and you'll learn everything
there is to know

just don't try to make sense of it
or it shall crumble

and the rocks will become
just rocks

and you will become
just flesh and bone

and life will return
to the stale world of
words, descriptions, definitions

———

mother nature will carry you
where she pleases

you may find salvation
you may find death

the trick is to *flow*
navigating her natural rhythms
like a bird on the wind
a surfer on a wave
a sailor on the open sea

there's a fine line
between playing safe
and playing smart

play too safe
and you risk reaching the destination
but missing the journey

we're all headed for the same place
we all die

the difference
is how you get there

———

happiness comes in all sorts of flavors
it has little to do with money
fame or success

do what makes you happy
and inevitably you'll become a happy person

do what makes you miserable
and a miserable person you become

the formula is simple
but our lives get so complex
that we forget about the simple things

the *important things*

———

can we ever get back to our playful
childlike, trusting selves?

how to disable this incessant judging
that contaminates our thoughts
and behaviors?

it's impossible to judge someone
until you step into their shoes
feel their world
see their unique points of view

each of us experiences reality
through different sets of eyes
different sets of circumstances

your circumstances define who you are
my circumstances define who i am

and neither of us is *wrong*

———

the secret to living a meaningful life?
do something well
really well

look at nature
and you'll find this to be true

birds master the art of flying
fish master the art of swimming
plants master the art of flowering

you won't find a dolphin
deliberating its life's purpose
it's to swim!

the better swimmer she becomes
the more she gets to eat
the less chance she has of being eaten
and the more fun she gets to have being a dolphin

humans no longer have
this inherent sense of purpose

our days of chasing food
and running from predators
are long behind us

the pursuit of fun
has been relegated to our free time
when we're finished doing
more *important things*

because of this
we no longer have a sole definition
of what it means to be human

there are just so many choices
this can be very exciting
and also quite terrifying

many become paralyzed with indecision
at the sheer vastness of possibility

constantly, we're being persuaded
to do this or do that

so much that we rarely stop to ask ourselves
what we actually *enjoy* doing

each of us has the ability to master something
but we must enjoy what we're mastering

if we do it for money or fame or recognition
or because we feel pressured
then mastering becomes a burden

there's no joy in the journey
because it's all about the destination

you might become proficient
but rarely will you find happiness

———

the world becomes unrecognizable
when we refuse to evolve with it

deeper we crawl into our caves
blocking out all light
except for what streams
through a glowing rectangle
in the center of the room

we become hypnotized by news
propaganda, biased facts

our world becomes filled
with endless problems
because that's all we see

we forget that all we must do is step outside
feel the sunshine on our face
the wind in our hair
and say:

my god
where have i been?

look at these arms
they still work!

look at my legs
they still walk!

look at this heart
it still beats!

look at that sun
it still shines!

———

people generally suffer
from one of two things:

a life too short
or a life too long

the average human now lives 72 years
that's a long time if we don't *evolve*

fortunately, there's no law that says
you have to be the same person today
as you were yesterday

———

change keeps us involved
it keeps us from getting dissociated or depressed
it keeps us alive

when we pursue meaningful activities
we don't have time to be depressed

we're not searching for artificial stimulants
because we're already high

wanting to feel high is natural
when we're continually learning
and experiencing new things
we are tuned into our natural state of ecstasy

there's enough to carry us through the day
through our lives

this state of being sharpens our minds
exercises our bodies
keeps our arteries clear

we become vibrant, happy earthlings

————

whether finding a cure for cancer
or learning to finger paint

the pursuit of meaningful activity
leads us toward fulfilling lives

with our eyes fixed
on a meaningful objective
we can handle any kind of weather

when we lose sight of our dreams
we get lost in the storms

———

security cannot be found
in an ever-changing world

economies collapse
jobs disappear
industries change

this so-called security we're chasing?
it is an illusion, a phantom, a ghost

life changes
and we must evolve with it

there's only one way to survive
this rapidly changing world

we must learn
to ride the tides

———

why attempt to control
that which we cannot control?

sounds like a good way
to end up in the loony bin

life is a sea of moments
a constant stream of nows
and then you die

the only thing you can control is *this* now
the only one that exists

what puts a smile on your face?
now do that

keep doing that until you're no longer smiling
now do something else

(repeat as necessary)

most of us can't live this way
because we're fully invested in *future* nows

this is like putting all your eggs in one basket

future nows are highly speculative
because there's no guarantee they'll ever come

furthermore, when tomorrow's now arrives
we shift our focus to more future nows

and so it goes...

when do we ever get to this elusive, future now
that we spend our entire lives preparing for?

that's right, *tomorrow*

———

when water flows down a sidewalk
it branches into different directions
following the paths of least resistance

in every situation
there are paths of least resistance

they key is cultivating our sense of navigation
so we flow effortlessly along these paths
without hesitation

we must become like water

———

when our sights are fixed
on a meaningful objective
our trajectory is clear

when we reach our goal
we must have a new destination awaiting
or we become aimless wanderers

always there must be
a point on the horizon
just out of reach
that we are navigating *towards*

everything in nature has direction
plants grow towards the sun
bees seek the nectar of flowers
salmon swim upriver to spawn

when we have direction
we become part of this harmonious dance

and nature guides us
where we want to go

———

the good thing about knowing
precisely what you want
is that your choices become limited

this kind of laser focus
uncovers opportunities
that others cannot see

———

there are two types
of people in this world:

those who say
'i can't'

and those who say
'how can i?'

this simple shift of words
changes everything

one closes a door
the other opens it

you can change a dead-end
into a gateway

simply by adjusting your *perspective*

———

nature teaches us to look
where others don't

it shows us magic beyond
all the strip malls and walmarts

we need connection with nature
like we need oxygen to breathe

otherwise we become suffocated
by whatever narrative surrounds us

———

sooner or later
we'll all face disappointments

illness, financial loss
death of loved ones, our own annihilation
these things cannot be avoided

they are *inescapable*

the key is to stop worrying about them
and start living each moment
with hallucinatory clarity

until we learn to enjoy
the ebbing and flowing of life

much of our time will be wasted
trying to avoid its unpleasantries

———

in any relationship
there is give and take

forget this
and you'll get eaten alive

respect nature's rhythms
and a lifetime love affair ensues

fight her
and life becomes a constant battle

we are here—
not as aliens
but as integral parts of the earth

removed as we've become
our once-deep relationship with mother nature
has been neglected and forgotten

we can rekindle our connection
by engaging with her elements

everything is a force
coming at us

it's our choice to either fight
or befriend those forces

if we fight them
we make enemies with mother nature

when we befriend them
a deep relationship ensues

with life itself

———

to chase security
is to chase death—

missing out on life
and all its great adventures

what is ultimate security?

no more wanting
no more needing
no more pain
no more struggle?

ultimate security is an empty promise
because it only exists in our demise

life is a sea of moments
you can't hold onto just one

we ride a good wave
and wish to stay on it forever

but you can't set anchor on a wave
waves come and go

yet the ocean lives on

———

i feel myself
envying the trees

they appear so perfectly content
with just the bark on their trunks
and the leaves on their branches

perhaps i was born with rose-colored glasses
but when i'm in the wilderness
all i see is perfection

i've seen a bobcat take down a rabbit
yet cannot observe a trace of ill intent

only divine transformation

―――――

back home...
my thoughts remain tightly wound
draining precious energy

but in the mountains...
there's no energy to spare
for such inconsequential things
as incessant thought

every ounce of power is needed
to push through this valley
and climb these peaks

it's a pilgrimage of sorts
this journey beyond the self
a spiritual practice, if you will

this is the reason i do these things
this must be why i follow these
pathways of desire

because beyond the next ridge
through the next drainage
past the farthest meadows and friendly pines
just a little further!

lies *the gateway to the soul*

———

silence, i'm learning
can be a destination in itself

in our chaotic world of incessant noise
silence feels uncommonly rich

out here in the forest
life is as simple as it gets

one foot in front of the other
is all that's required

this, i can deal with
no matter how my muscles burn
and my stomach rumbles

for hours, i continue the slow march
steadily gaining altitude
onward, forward, upward

toward the lofty goal
of *nothing in particular*

———

i've been too busy thinking
always thinking

lost inside myself
and my thoughts

too far gone to realize
that what i seek
what i long for
is already here

i just needed to lose the baggage
put down the gadgets
and *take a long walk*

———

emergence

when the last drops
of thought have fallen
we are able to truly see
through *the eyes of the world*

———

the secret to life is *now*
in every living moment
whatever that moment may look like

when i finally stop, look around, and see
actually see for the first time
all the grace and beauty in this world
i realize something profound

the beauty has been here all along
waiting for me to get out of my head
and into life

———

we must have escapes
emergency exits
portals to secret worlds
where we can sneak away for a while
reclaim our souls

without escapes
we'd surely go insane

it could be a forest meadow
a neighborhood park
a secluded beach

perhaps it's the pub
the coffee shop
the library
the casino

or a sailboat on the wind
a fish on the line
a surfboard on a breaking wave

a break from life
whatever reality you've found yourself
trapped in at the moment

———

i was born to walk the earth
experience the beauty of this planet
and witness the magic and splendor
of all things

to be overwhelmed by a ray of sunlight
touched by an encounter with a frog
mystified by the texture of a rock wall

i was born to splash through the creeks
sing through the canyons
laugh with the squirrels

just like i did as a child
in the woods behind our family's home

i was born to be a kid
not take life too seriously
or get sidetracked by anything
that ties me down to the life of bills
shiny new toys, status and pavement

———

i am here for an instant
a spark of observation
the flash of a camera lens

i've been given a precious gift—
the rare opportunity to capture
this precise moment
of beauty and perfection
at this exact pinpoint in history

it's a *miracle*

like an ocean wave suspended in time
i've stepped right into the photo
and been granted an entire lifetime
to explore its fine blue edges
sculpted arcs, and sensual curves

the wave will crash
this i know all too well
it will become the ocean again

but for now!

with such a rare opportunity
how can i possibly justify
not seeing all there is to see?

every beach, every mountain
every river, every trail

i want to see it all!
there is so much beauty

and only *so much time*

———

when i die i'll return to the soil
to be born again

perhaps next time as a flower
a tree, a frog, or if i'm lucky
a high soaring bird

we come from the earth
we return to the earth
it happens over and over and over

you might say, we *are* the earth

we've only to step away from our world
of plastic and concrete to understand

———

how much better
to simply let things
be as they are

and witness life
with a sense of humor?

it is quite *silly* after all

———

why should we ever stop having fun?

i plan to have fun
until it's no longer possible

then i'll surely be ready to move on
recycle this old body back to the earth
see what's next

how can it not be great?
perhaps even greater than this life

until then i plan to have as much fun
as humanly possible

———

staying in the *flow*
this is the key

remaining in touch with my body
and the moon, the stars, sunrise, sunset

and remembering, knowing—
that it's all me

that the crystal clear waters
of the desert canyons will still flow
even if i'm not here to witness them

that the moon, the stars
the constellations, and the planets
will still make their journey across the night sky
even if there's a roof over my head

that i must only stop, look up, and look around
to realize that everything
absolutely everything is *beautiful*

———

wilderness is the place
to understand the universe

life, death, love, hate
beauty, darkness

there's an order to all this chaos
i see it so clearly now

———

we are here to frolic the hillsides
dance with the flowers
run with the squirrels
sing with the songbirds
play with the dolphins

we are here to *love*
not just other humans
but everything on this planet

we are the earth's children
the mountains, oceans, forests, and animals
they are our *kin*

———

the secret to life
is having fun

not convinced?
go out into a field
and watch a hawk for about an hour

or paddle out into the ocean
and watch dolphins
or chipmunks in a city park
or butterflies

imagine for a moment
we could communicate with these creatures
try to reason with them
that life isn't about having fun
try explaining that they should focus
on something a bit more serious

teach them that life
is about hard work and discipline
tell the chipmunks to stop goofing off
and start earning a living

what might they say
about this line of thought?

what might they try to teach us?

———

when life becomes
a constant expression of gratitude

you'll know the
true meaning of happiness

———

you are here on earth
to fulfill a fundamental task:
to be 100 percent uniquely you

no matter what you do with your life
your perspective matters
that's why you are here

your perspective, for better or worse
is something we can all learn from

you make the world a better place
in ways you cannot even imagine

———

isn't the point to have fun?

isn't that the whole point
and nothing but the point?

shouldn't we be spending our days
celebrating the unfathomable notion
that somehow we get to be humans
in this whole shebang?

how uncanny that we woke up today as people?
the whole thing is utterly ridiculous
like waking up one morning
and realizing you're a zebra
or a penguin, or a giraffe

as homo sapiens
we can surf and sail
and dance and bake pastries

we can create art and play music
and write poetry

the possibilities are endless!
the candy bowl is full

choose a flavor

———

when we're young
we want to do everything

we go through these phases
where we want to be astronauts
dancers, movie stars, magicians

the world is an ocean
of opportunity

our futures bright
as the noonday sun

we can recreate this experience as adults
by opening new pathways in the brain

those opportunities—
they're still endless!

all that's required
is trying something new

———

a wise fisherman once told me
it's not the fish he's after

it's the *ineffable*
that connection to something greater

that feeling that reminds us
we're still alive

———

life is not a journey
to a mountaintop

but a world
of endless peaks to explore

rippling beyond the horizon
as far as the eyes can see

———

use those precious vacation days
sick days, holidays, personal days

rent a cabin in the woods
or a bungalow by the sea

or better yet, head to your nearest wilderness
and start walking with nothing but a backpack
a sleeping bag, perhaps a bag of nuts

turn off the world for three or four days
and listen to that chatter inside your mind

that nonstop reel of chaotic noise
that controls your every thought and desire

watch and observe these strange images—
which are not your own
and have little to do with who you are

watch them from afar
like you're *eavesdropping*

until all that noise seems so bizarre
so abstract, so alien
that you no longer identify with it

then watch it drift away
like leaves on a fall day

———

my flesh is fleeting like a wave
but i am eternal like the sea

in this revelation
i realize that i *can* surf that eternal wave

because each time a wave dies
another is born

they just keep coming
the rhythm never stops

there's so much beauty
that i want to experience

my biggest fear is dying
before i get to see it all

when i'm outside in nature
that fear disappears

i simply relax into enjoying
what's happening now

because *now* is all there ever is to see

———

when we connect deeply
with our environment
we no longer feel separate
from the world that surrounds us

this is where transformation occurs

we begin to see the world and all its forces
as extensions of ourselves

no longer are we strangers in a strange land
but integral parts of a greater force

we develop a second nature
similar to a sailor navigating a ship
during a storm

life becomes about honing our skills—
an endeavor that keeps us
fully engrossed in the world

whether flying a plane, sailing a ship
or knitting a wool blanket

it's *all* about navigation

———

when water gets stagnant
it becomes polluted

eventually
it dries up completely

we are not so different

―――――

our lives are pulses
in an eternal rhythm

we come and go
like ocean waves

while you read these words
thousands are being born
just as thousands are dying

the earth produces humans
like it grows oranges and tomatoes

death and birth are part of the process
and it's all part of a great rhythm
that started with the beginning of time

it never stops

we are not separate from this rhythm
we *are* the rhythm

———

our lives are tiny sparks of observation
and this is entirely *the point*

we needn't fear death
because these sparks go on indefinitely
a kind of pulsing electricity
that never ceases to exist

from this perspective
it's easy to see we are part of a greater process

to fear death would be like holding a funeral
for an ocean wave

waves are part of the rhythm
and the rhythm goes on!

———

do you cry
each time you eat a banana?

of course not
the banana is a repeatable act
and so are you

next time you might have
red hair, or dark skin
or you might be covered in fur
or scales, or feathers

how boring might it be
to live forever?

———

life dances—

it twists and twirls
and boogies and hops

it bounces and wiggles
and flickers and flops

it rocks and rolls
and trips and tumbles

it jiggles and wobbles
and frollicks and fumbles

you can't *stop the rhythm*

———

i am a different person
in the wilderness

my doors of perception
are completely open to the landscape

no longer
am i sleepwalking

i'm a thousand percent myself

in the city
we're completely maxed out on *mind stuff*
our brains think we're dying

i suppose we *are* all dying
some just faster than others

———

who are we to dwell on the past
thinking it better or worse
than this sparkling moment before our eyes?

what we are witnessing
ladies and gentlemen
is nothing less than the great story of life!

who are we to judge it
as anything less than perfection?

sixty-six million years ago
when an asteroid hit the earth
triggering an earthquake
that covered the planet
with dust and darkness
wiping out the dinosaurs
was it not perfect?

when a similar demise occurs
to our own species
will it not be perfect then?

who are we to impose our judgments
upon the universe's great unfolding?

surely, she has plans much larger
than our imposed human agendas

———

as our modernized culture
is slowly beginning to realize
less really is more

simplification allows us to experience
the world with clearer eyes and purer souls
untainted by the fear of losing
our life savings

isn't this the primary source
of today's worries?

as soon as we get our hands
on even the smallest pile of cash
we guard it with our lives
basing every decision on protecting
these little scraps of paper

just remember
you can't take it with you

———

at the end of our days
all we have are our experiences

it costs nothing to witness
the sparkling dew on a blade of grass
or the snow wisps
that decorate a mountain top
or the morning sunlight
illuminating the walls of a towering canyon

our ancestors experienced such luxuries
on a daily basis with untainted eyes

no wonder they saw these natural
landscapes as holy

they hold a majesty
beyond anything money can buy

———

does knowing the anatomy of an oak tree
mean you fully understand it?

or does sleeping beside it
night after night?

naming and categorizing things
can be an interesting endeavor
but it hinders our ability
to understand the world as it truly is

as such, my life has become an exercise
in learning how to see nature
for the sake of *itself*

to look beyond the human usefulness
of something and see what the mountains see

unclouded by words, thoughts
names, labels

———

in the forest
i tap into a language
much older and more sophisticated
than what's available in our human vocabulary

to understand it
my mind must be silent

open to receiving
whatever messages might arrive

———

what would the earth be like
without humans?

would it be more perfect
than it is now?
less perfect?

these are difficult questions

each year, more species are becoming extinct
meanwhile, new ones are developing

this is not the end of creation
but just the beginning

the big bang happened
only a moment ago

the universe is still expanding
faster than the speed of light

i have no doubt that the future
will turn out just as it's supposed to

whether humans are part of that equation
remains to be seen

regardless, it shall be no *less perfect*
than ever before

———

you go to a concert these days
and people are watching it
through their smartphones

as if their video of the moment
will be better than the real thing

social media is full of such
lost moments in time

never will life be better
than it is *right now*

never truer, never richer
never more alive
than this very moment

constantly, we put up barriers
between ourselves and the divine moment
flashing before our eyes

as if we're ashamed
to look god squarely in the face

what are we so afraid of?

———

one day it happens—
and it hits us like a sack of bricks

we see the grand canyon
or witness the birth of a child
or have a close call with death

for once, we can't look away
and it brings us to our knees

we don't know whether to laugh
or scream or cry

such divinity is difficult to contain
but it's worth knowing

because from this place, we are born
and to this place, we shall return
when our final moments come

why not become friends with it now
while we're still alive?

———

when we surrender
to the present moment
the universe guides us to all the right places

decisions are just decisions
either answer is correct
just choose

when we fight the present moment
the universe turns against us

nothing goes our way
every decision is wrong

life becomes a *struggle*

———

when i'm a ninety-year-old man
with only stories left to tell

i'll look back on this life
and remember:

ah, those were the days
young and free
alive with dreams as big as the world
what i wouldn't give to go back there...

then in an instant
like magic!
here i am

the old man gets his wish again

i know of no better way to live my life
than from the perspective
of my ninety-year-old self

because i always know
what he would say

and it's never:

you should have worked more
saved more, bought a nicer car
a bigger house, been more responsible

———

true magic
exists

it just remains
hidden

not in the far reaches
of our imagination

but right here on *earth*

———

i find myself the most alive
when words and thoughts subside

that's where life begins

to truly understand a place like this
we must lay our thinking minds aside
and simply breathe in the magic

surrender to the mystery

———

like dancers in sequins
the cottonwoods dazzle and sparkle
against an illuminated backdrop
of glowing red sandstone

such a glory to witness!

what's so comforting
so reassuring
so gratifying
is the fact that this happens every day
whether i'm here or not

beauty remains
perfection exists!

unfathomable
unconditional
long before we ever existed
long after we are gone

this place *remains*

———

a skilled sailor tacks slowly upwind
until it shifts in her favor
then she seizes the opportunity to fly

we can fly too
but sometimes we must tack
until things shift in our favor

if the winds never change
we may need to change course altogether

the key is to remain fluid
making *subtle adjustments* along the way

———

when i die i'll become the dirt
nourishing the plants and trees
blooming into fields of wildflowers
in the spring

i'll flow with the creeks and rivers
replenishing the lakes
evaporating into the clouds

then i'll rain down upon the earth
filling the aquifers and wells
nourishing a thirsty child on a hot summer day

and i'll go on, and on, and on...

―――――

there is wisdom in anarchy
precision in chaos

everything in nature is in its perfect place
yet precisely out of order

straight lines and boxes—
the world growing tired of them

correct grammar
a complete sentence?

i don't want a complete sentence
i want to feel!

words that pierce my soul
give me that one magically placed word
that stops me dead in my tracks
forces me to stop reading
and *tremble*

transcendence!
is that too much to ask?

———

alone in a sea of stars
reflecting off the water
out into infinity

i can no longer differentiate
between water and sky

there is no end

———

our human sense
of separateness is unique

it must be *unlearned*
to reconnect with the rest of nature

in wilderness
our way of thinking is the exception
not the rule

so it's easier to let it fall away

the sooner we let go of what's false
the easier we can get down to what's real

how much better to be connected!

the feeling is always the same
it's a *welcome home*

like i've been away so long
asleep in a coma or false dream state

a caged bird set free

———

i'll never take for granted the privilege to walk
one foot in front of the other
in the direction of my own choosing

the opportunity to get lost
so that i might find myself again

each time i'm surprised at what i find

wilderness is my church
my teacher, my mentor, my psychologist
my mother, my savior

the school of life
where we learn not from books
nor words, nor lectures

a classroom where we learn
not from that which thinks
but that which *knows*

the lesson is truth itself

i can no more explain this
than i can explain the sparkle in a baby's eyes
or falling in love for the first time
or the agony of heartbreak

the loss of a child
the death of a dream

good, bad, or ugly—
truth is undeniable

it cannot be run from
nor grasped by the mind
only experienced by the soul

truth is what i come out here to find

———

a prolonged detachment from the familiar
is required to achieve the unknown

the longer i remove myself
from the workings of mankind

the better i'm able to hear
the whispers in the wind
the voices in the cottonwoods
the murmurs in the streams

these sounds—
they intertwine
wrapping around each other
like serpents in a ritual dance

with a beauty that touches my soul intimately
plucking the strings of my very own heart
vibrating inside my chest
causing me to weep

———

it's not just her beauty
i wish to capture
but her message
her mere reason for existence

i love her for her beauty
i'd be lying if i said i did not

her beauty is intoxicating, powerful
leaving me speechless
weak in the knees
unable to express my infatuation
my devotion

she *is* beauty

yet beyond her beauty
lies the most profound spiritual presence
i've ever known

———

sometimes we must pull in the anchor
leave the harbor
cast off into the unknown sea

———

when the world is ending
do we wallow in fear or have a party?

i find it incredibly exciting
that we get to witness such change
in our lifetimes

we must remember
that mother nature ebbs and flows
like the tides

it's all part of
the great happening

who are we to say
it's not going perfectly as planned?

if we could only step back, refocus
and see that we're not
the main characters in the play

we're barely *supporting roles*

in due time our buildings and houses
sidewalks and superhighways
strip malls and walmarts
will be brushed away
like dust from a rose

but the show—
the show goes on!

i am a committed student of nature
and intend to spend as much time
as possible on my thesis

so long as mother nature is my teacher
i know i'll never lose focus

this lifelong assignment
is paramount to my evolution

there's a lifetime of wisdom
to be learned

my dedication is strong enough
to handle any of life's *distractions*
that might get in the way

———

nature is full of poetry and metaphor
her wisdom is as necessary
to our understanding of the world as science

there's always something new to comprehend
beyond facts, labels, charts

things you can only see
with the mind's eye

those who spend countless hours outdoors
will understand well enough what i mean

in mother nature's classroom
we are permitted to remain children
all our lives

for she can only be imperfectly
comprehended

the more we learn
the more we realize—

how *little* we truly understand

———

beyond the walls of civilization
lies something profoundly more human
than anything in our civilized world

when i go to the wilderness
i discover my truest self

i get to die for a moment
experience my shangri-la
and become reborn with new eyes
with which to view the world

———

i don't know what happens when we die
but i imagine it must be something
of a coming home

fortunately
we don't have to die to experience this

there is heaven right here on earth
come on in, see for yourself

hop in a car, hitch a ride
or simply start walking
just get here!

you will be cleansed
you will be renewed
and given a new perspective on life

ready for the next chapter
born again into the world

yes! wilderness can do all of that!

———

the way out of delusion
is through connection

with a tree,
a flower, a bird, a rock

when we learn to see nature
as our kin

we will wake from this
long strange dream

and the world will become *alive again*

———

here i am
this is me

this is who i am

———————

my passing is as fleeting
as a falling snowflake

my existence as temporary
as a flea buzzing in your ear
and just like that

i'll be *gone*

————

enjoy this book?
write a review!

---

if you've enjoyed my book, the best compliment you can give is writing a review. as a self-published indie author, i don't have the advertising power of a major publishing firm. but you can make a big difference.

honest reviews help other readers find me. it only takes five minutes, and the review can be as short as you like.

if you'd like to leave a review on **amazon.com**, search for my title, click on customer reviews, then click write a customer review. simple as that.

thank you very much

nature book series
(5 part series)

---

explore the alpine peaks of the rocky mountains, the sandstone slot canyons of the colorado plateau, the lush mangrove islands of the florida keys, and the winter backcountry of the san juan mountains in scott stillman's nature book series.

have you read all the books in the series?

- wilderness, the gateway to the soul
- nature's silent message
- i don't want to grow up
- oceans of my mind
- solace of winter

(books can be read in any order)

sign up for my mailing list and you'll gain access to:

- free previews of each book in the series
- my ongoing blog posts
- exclusive photographs
- 10% off your first order

you can sign up for my mailing list at
www.scottstillmanblog.com

save wild utah!

southern utah wilderness alliance (suwa)
suwa is the only nonpartisan, nonprofit organization working full time to defend utah's redrock canyons from oil and gas development, unnecessary road construction, rampant off-road vehicle use, and other threats to utah's wilderness-quality lands. their power comes from people like you from across the nation who want to protect this irreplaceable heritage for all americans.

if you'd like to get involved, please find them at **www.suwa.org**

SOUTHERN UTAH WILDERNESS ALLIANCE

about the author

scott stillman is the author of the #1 international bestselling book, *i don't want to grow up.*

he is a writer who helps others realize there is life outside a traditional 9-5 career. scott's books provide refreshing insight, showing that you don't have to be rich to live your passions.

he and his wife, valerie, have lived in a truck camper and found unconventional ways to fund their travels and stay on the path of adventure, freedom, and fun.

born in ohio, scott moved to colorado, in 2003. wandering mountains, deserts, and oceans, he records his journeys with pen and notebook, writing primarily about our spiritual connection to nature.

as our culture continues to remove itself from the natural world, scott's books provide refreshing insight, showing that there's life outside the regimen—hope beyond the pavement.

you can find his blog and online home at:
scottstillmanblog.com
facebook.com/scottstillmanblog

if the mood strikes, send him an email at:
scottstillmanauthor@gmail.com